POETRY 2

Marbles in my pocket

Series Editor
MOIRA ANDREW

Macmillan Education

'For David'

Selection © Moira Andrew 1986
Illustrations © Macmillan Education Ltd 1986

First published 1986

Published by
MACMILLAN EDUCATION LTD
Houndmills, Basingstoke, Hampshire RG21 2XS
and London
Companies and representatives
throughout the world

Typeset by
Acorn Bookwork, Salisbury, Wilts

Printed in Hong Kong

British Library Cataloguing in Publication Data
Poetry 2: Marbles in my pocket.—(Junior
poetry anthologies; 2)
1. English poetry—20th century
I. Andrew, Moira   II. Series
821'.914'08   PR1174
ISBN 0-333-39202-7

Acknowledgements

The editor and publishers wish to thank the following who have kindly given permission for the use of copyright material:

George Allen & Unwin Ltd for 'A Small Dragon' by Brian Patten from **Notes to the Hurrying Man**. L. T. Baynton for 'Our Street'. Adam and Charles Black (Publishers) Ltd for 'Poem of Solitary Delight' from **Bric a Brac** by P. Blakely. The Bodley Head for 'Three Hole' by John Agard from **I Din Do Nuttin**. Alan Brownjohn for 'Chameleon' from **Brownjohn's Beasts**. Carcanet Press Ltd for 'Blue Toboggans' by Edwin Morgan from **Poems of Thirty Years** by Edwin Morgan, 1982. Tony Charles for 'Rabbit and Dragon' in **Schools' Poetry Review** published by Schools' Poetry Association. Kay Cornish for 'The Spaceman' and 'Rain', John Cotton for 'Fireworks', 'Christmas Day in the Suburbs' and 'Exploring the Rock Pool'. Andre Deutsch Ltd for 'Autumn' by Roy Fuller from **Seen Grandpa Lately**; 'Who Rolled in the Mud?' and 'Father Says' from **Mind Your Own Business** by Michael Rosen. Elaine Eveleigh for 'Michael'. Faber and Faber Ltd for 'My Papa's Waltz' from **The Collected Poems of Theodore Roethke**; 'My Brother Bert' from **Meet My Folks** by Ted Hughes. John Fairfax for 'Upon a Time' and 'Three Dragons'. Farrar, Straus & Giroux Inc. for 'crickets' from **Small Poems** by Valerie Worth, 1972. Alexander Franklin for 'Open Windows'. Mrs Dorothy Gibson for 'A Memory' by the late Douglas Gibson. Pamela Gillilan for 'Plot' and 'Robin'. Rumer Godden for the translation of 'The Prayer of the Little Ducks' from **Prayers from the Ark** by Carmen Bernos de Gasztold. David Harmer for 'Wet Playtime', 'The Tunnel' and 'Bus Route'. Miranda Harris for 'Song'. Michael Henry for 'Cloud Cuckoo' and 'Shrove Tuesday'. David Higham Associates Ltd on behalf of Eleanor Farjeon for 'The Elm Tree' from **Silver Sand and Snow** published by Michael Joseph Ltd on behalf of Elizabeth Jennings for 'The Secret Brother'; on behalf of Russell Hoban for 'Esmé on Her Brother's Bicycle', and on behalf of Charles Causley for 'Legend' and 'Green Man in the Garden'. Dr Philip Hobsbaum for 'The Ice Skaters' from **Coming Out Fighting** (1969). Hodder & Stoughton Ltd for 'Unknown' and 'Trip to London' from **The Corn Growing** by Leonard Clark and 'The Singing Time' from **The Singing Time** by Leonard Clark. The Hogarth Press Ltd for 'Frogs' from **Surroundings** by Norman McCaig, and for 'July Day Spectacular' from **The White Bird** by Norman McCaig. Geoffrey Holloway for 'Please to Remember'. Libby Houston for 'All Change!' and 'Rhymes for a Blue-bottle'. Olwyn Hughes on behalf of Ted Hughes for 'Fiesta Melons' by Sylvia Plath from **Collected Poems** published by Faber & Faber Ltd. Copyright © 1971 and 1981 by Ted Hughes. Paul Johnson for 'An Old Lady'. Jean Kenward for 'Candle'. James Kirkup for 'The Bird Fancier' from **Refusal to Conform: Last and First Poems** published by Oxford University Press. Brian Levison for 'Four Legends about Christmas Eve'. Little, Brown and Company for 'Cat and the Weather' by May Swenson from **New and Selected Things Taking Place** by May Swenson and for 'The Greedy Giant' from **Tirra Lirra** by Laura E. Richards (1932). Copyright © renewed by Hamilton Richards. Francis Lovell for 'The Double'. Wes Magee for 'The Witch's Brew'. Hughes Massie Ltd on behalf of Langston Hughes for 'Dream Variation'. Madeline Mayne for 'Bonfire Night' and 'The House on the Hill'. Ian McMillan for 'When my Dad Came Home from the Sea' and 'Batman' by John Turner from **Versewagon** and 'The First Bus of the Day' by George Inkerman. Penguin Books Ltd for 'Pockets' and 'Bad Dog' by Brian Lee from **Late Home** by Brian Lee (Kestrel Books 1976). Copyright © 1976 by Brian Lee; 'The Hardest Thing in the World to Do' by Michael Rosen from **You Tell Me** by Roger McGough and Michael Rosen; 'Night Walk' by Max Fatchen from **Songs for My Dog and Other People** by Max Fatchen (Kestrel Books 1980). Copyright © 1980 by Max Fatchen. A. D. Peters & Co. Ltd on behalf of Roger McGough for 'Uncle Terry was a Skydiver' from **Sporting Relations** published by Eyre Methuen Ltd. Laurence Pollinger Ltd on behalf of Kenneth Patchen for 'The Magical Mouse' from **Collected Poems**. Peter Mortimer for 'Janitor Jeffries'. Brian Moses for 'Dig to Australia'. Judith Nicholls for 'Night' and 'Late'. Patricia Pogson for 'Eatscape' and 'Cat'. Malcolm Povey for 'Questions'. Felix Redmill for 'At Peace'. Martin Secker & Warburg Ltd for 'The Round Pond' from **Close Relatives** by Vicki Feaver. Eric Slayter for 'Questions and Answers' and 'Changing Times'. Myfanwy Thomas for 'Tall Nettles' from **Collected Poems** by Edward Thomas published by Faber and Faber Ltd. Mrs A. M. Walsh for 'Journey Home' from **The Roundabout by the Sea** by John Walsh published by Oxford University Press. Donna Wasiczko for 'Bananas' and 'View over a Fence'.

Every effort has been made to trace all the copyright holders but if any have been inadvertently overlooked the publishers will be pleased to make the necessary arrangement at the first opportunity.

Illustrations by the students of Middlesex Polytechnic and St. Martin's School of Art

CONTENTS

Marbles in my pocket

Marbles in my pocket!
Winter-time's begun!
Marbles in my pocket
That rattle when I run!

Heavy in my pocket
On the way to school;
Smooth against my fingers,
Round and hard and cool;

Marbles in my pocket,
Blue and green and red,
And some are yellow-golden,
And some are brown instead

Marbles in the playground,
Big and little ring –
Oh, I like playing marbles,
But that's a different thing.

Marbles in my pocket,
Smooth within my hand,
That's the part that's nicest;
Do you understand?

Marbles in my pocket
To rattle when I run!
For winter days are here again,
And marble-time's begun!

Lydia Pender

Pockets

'Come on, where have you put it?
Turn out your pockets . . .
If you can't find it,
You'll never get home.'

An old grey hanky,
An Irish ha'penny,
A coil of string,
And an old brass ring –
A peppermint chew
(Half for me, half for you),
A piece of wire,
A dinky-car tyre,
My bicycle clips
And two poker-chips,
An old rubber, gone hard,
And a cigarette card
(Extremely rare) –
No, it's not there.

'Well, where *have* you put it? –
Try the left-hand pocket.
No wonder you've lost it.
The bus hasn't gone yet.'

A big paper clip
And a lead battleship,
An elastic band
And a pinch of sand
Still there from last summer,
A pencil sharpener,

Glass marbles, a pin,
A box for keeping things in –
Empty – a whistle
And a tiny pistol
From a Christmas cracker,
A bit of sherbet sucker,
My two old front teeth –
And underneath –

I've got it, I've got it –
My five penny bit.

'The bus still hasn't gone,
Be quick now, and run!

And now that we're on,
Swap you something of yours
For something of mine.'

'No. No one can have them.
They're mine, they're all mine.'

Brian Lee

The Secret Brother

Jack lived in the green-house
When I was six,
With glass and with tomato plants,
Not with slates and bricks.

I didn't have a brother
Jack became mine.
Nobody could see him,
He never gave a sign.

Just beyond the rockery,
By the apple-tree,
Jack and his old mother lived,
Only for me.

With a tin telephone
Held beneath the sheet,
I would talk to Jack each night.
We would never meet.

Once my sister caught me,
Said, 'He isn't there.
Down among the flower-pots
Cramm the gardener

Is the only person.'
I said nothing, but
Let her go on talking.
Yet I moved Jack out.

He and his old mother
Did a midnight flit.
No one knew his number:
I had altered it.

Only I could see
The sagging washing-line
And my brother making
Our own secret sign

Elizabeth Jennings

My Brother Bert

Pets are the Hobby of my Brother Bert.
He used to go to school with a Mouse in his shirt.

His Hobby it grew, as some hobbies will,
And grew and GREW and GREW until –

Oh don't breathe a word, pretend you haven't heard.
A simply appalling thing has occurred –

The very thought makes me iller and iller:
Bert's brought home a gigantic Gorilla!

If you think that's really not such a scare,
What if it quarrels with his Grizzly Bear?

You still think you could keep your head?
What if the Lion from under the bed

And the four Ostriches that deposit
Their football eggs in his bedroom closet

And the Aardvark out of his bottom drawer
All danced out and joined in the Roar?

What if the Pangolins were to caper
Out of their nests behind the wallpaper?

With the fifty sorts of Bats
That hang on his hatstand like old hats,

And out of a shoebox the excitable Platypus
Along with the Ocelot or Jungle-Cattypus?

The Wombat, the Dingo, the Gecko, the Grampus –
How they would shake the house with their Rumpus!

Not to forget the Bandicoot
Who would certainly peer from his battered old boot.

Why it could be a dreadful day,
And what Oh what would the neighbours say!

Ted Hughes

Esmé on her Brother's Bicycle

One foot on, one foot pushing, Esmé starting off beside
Wheels too tall to mount astride,
Swings the off leg forward featly,
Clears the high bar nimbly, neatly,
With a concentrated frown
Bears the upper pedal down
As the lower rises, then
Brings her whole weight round again,
Leaning forward, gripping tight,
With her knuckles showing white,
Down the road goes, fast and small,
Never sitting down at all.

Russell Hoban

Dig to Australia

It was late
& Ray said we'd have to wait
till tomorrow
to dig to Australia . . .

Instead we watched TV
& tried to think how deep
we'd need to sink the hole
to break through.

But when it came to digging,
it was heavy & hard
& much further
than we'd thought.

Then late in the day
& still no kangaroos,
we left it,
large & wet & treacherous,
till out for coal
in the blackout night
Ray's dad discovered our hole . . .

And after he'd wiped
the mud from his clothes,
he warned if we ever dug again
he'd fill us in himself!

While his wife told how once
she'd dug for victory,
but no further.

Brian Moses

Who rolled in the mud?

Who rolled in the mud
behind the garage door?
Who left footprints
across the kitchen floor?

I know a dog whose nose is cold
I know a dog whose nose is cold

Who chased raindrops
down the windows?
Who smudged the glass
with the end of his nose?

I know a dog with a cold in his nose
I know a dog with a cold in his nose

Who wants a bath
and a tuppenny ha'penny biscuit?
Who wants to bed down
in his fireside basket?

Me, said Ranzo
I'm the dog with a cold.

Michael Rosen

Bad Dog

All day long, Bones hasn't been seen
– But now he comes slinking home
Smelling of ditches and streams
And pastures and pinewoods and loam
And tries to crawl under my bed.
His coat is caked with mud,
And one of his ears drips blood.
Nobody knows where he's been.

'Who did it?' they ask him, 'who . . . ?
He'll have to be bathed . . . the sinner . . .
Pack him off to his basket . . .
You *bad dog*, you'll get no dinner . . .'
And he cowers, and rolls an eye.
Tomorrow, I *won't* let him go –
But he licks my hand, and then – oh,
How I wish that I had been too.

Brian Lee

Night Walk

What are you doing away up there
On your great long legs in the lonely air?
  Come down here, where the scents are sweet,
  Swirling around your great, wide feet.

How can you know of the urgent grass
And the whiff of the wind that will whisper and pass
  Or the lure of the dark of the garden hedge
  Or the trail of a cat on the road's black edge?

What are you doing away up there
On your great long legs in the lonely air?
  You miss so much at your great, great height
  When the ground is full of the smells of night.

Hurry then, quickly, and slacken my lead
For the mysteries speak and the messages speed
  With the talking stick and the stone's slow mirth
  That four feet find on the secret earth.

Max Fatchen

Unknown

Not a footprint to be found,
Nothing left upon the sand,
Only silence all around
On the water and the land.

When rose up the harvest moon
He came in with foaming tide,
Just a green and black balloon,
Gashes on his face and side.

Leonard Clark

Moon Thoughts

The moon is a ripe pumpkin
waiting for Hallowe'en teeth.

It is a yellow gumdrop
sucked enough to see through.

It is a slice of lemon, sour
in a ginger beer sky.

It is an antique Hunter watch
worn across night's stomach.

It is a brass button lost
from some sailor's pea jacket.

The moon is far enough away
to fantasise about, despite

Apollo and man's long steps.

Moira Andrew

Eatscape

mouldy orange moon
with tacky cloudpatches
are you really
from the same rack
as last week's
clean sliced lemon?

Patricia Pogson

Sky-silk

Wrapped in sky-silk
  Lies the moon
Ringed around
  Light a light-cocoon.

When she breaks
  Her yellow ring,
Look for a moth
  With a golden wing!

L. H. Allen

The Double

I hung my slip
On the line to dry

I hung myself
On a tree close by;

The stars came out
But said not a word –

Watched and waited
Like small, quiet birds;

The moon came past,
With one silver sigh

Breathed on us both
Her ice-cold 'why'?

Frances Lovell

Night

There's a dark, dark wood
inside my head
where the night owl cries;
where clambering roots
catch at my feet
where fox and bat
and badger meet
and night has eyes.

There's a dark, dark wood
inside my head
of oak and ash and pine;
where the clammy grasp
of a beaded web
can raise the hairs
on a wanderer's head
as he stares alone
from his mossy bed
and feels
the chill of his spine.

There's a dark, dark wood
inside my head
where the spider weaves;
where the rook rests
and the pale owl nests,
where moonlit bracken
spikes the air
and the moss is covered,
layer upon layer,
by a thousand fallen leaves.

Judith Nicholls

The House on the Hill

It was built years ago
by someone quite manic
and sends those who go there
away in blind panic.
They tell tales of horrors
that can injure or kill
designed by the madman
who lived on the Hill.

    If you visit the House on the Hill for a dare
    remember my words . . . 'There are dangers. Beware!'

The piano's white teeth,
when you plonk out a note,
will bite off your fingers
then reach for your throat.
The living room curtains
– long, heavy, and black –
will wrap you in cobwebs
if you're slow to step back.

    When you enter the House on the Hill for a dare
    remember my words . . . 'There are dangers. Beware!'

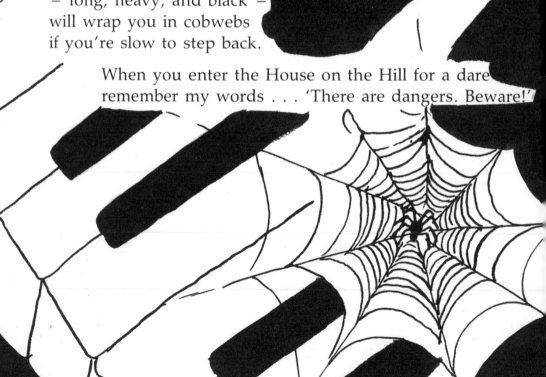

The fridge in the kitchen
has a self-closing door.
If it knocks you inside
then you're ice cubes . . . for sure.
The steps to the cellar
are littered with bones,
and up from the darkness
drift creakings and groans.

> If you go to the House on the Hill for a dare
> remember my words . . . 'There are dangers. Beware!'

Turn on the hot tap
and the bathroom will flood
not with gallons of water
but litres of blood.
The rocking-chair's arms
can squeeze you to death.
A waste of time shouting
as you run . . . out . . . of . . . breath.

> Don't say you weren't warned, or told to take care
> when you entered the House on the Hill . . .
> for a dare.

Wes Magee

An Old Soldier

Riding on a skinny horse,
he
comes dimly from the wood
and out of the morning mist
and returns dimly into the mist.

Day after day
he is carried unsteadily,
he knows not where:
on his sword there is
a little dust,
a little rust,
a little frost,
a little brightness,
a little blood shining in the morning sun.

Anon.

Please to Remember

He calls to see us every year
when he wants a change of clothes.
Mum's cold fingers take the hint
and she begins to sew.

Round the bottom of Dad's pyjamas,
round the sleeves of his old shirt;
straw and rags pushed down inside –
and a hat from Uncle Bert.

Sticks for arms, sticks for legs,
a walking stick across his knee,
punchball head, button eyes –
a nicer guy you couldn't see.

First he trundles round the streets
stuffed in his wheelbarrow,
catching coppers in his hat
like bread chucked for a sparrow.

Next, he'll find a house in a field, wood
wooden, with a nice position;
sit on the roof and crack on
he's a fire-eating magician.

Start by eating his head off
then have a bath in the stuff –
scrub his arms and legs so hard
they drop off

Then he'll wriggle down on his bottom,
sit in a blazing tyre, somersault for fun
and when we turn round to look again
– heypresto – he's gone!

But we don't worry. We know
next season sure as smoke
he'll be round again, to nudge us on
and get Mum's cold fingers going.

Geoffrey Holloway

Fireworks

First there was the eager looking forward
As hoarded in the safety of biscuit tins
Those bright cardboard buds awaited their flowering.
When, at a match's touch came
The sudden and immediate joy of crackle and colour
And the rocket's fiery upward rush.
Then last, the early morning's pleasure
(The night's smoke still on the air)
Of searching for the spent cases,
The charred and burnt-out husks,
The scorched rocket dew-drenched on its stick.
Something that might actually have soared
As high as our hopes.

John Cotton

Bonfire Night

Flash, bang,
Rockets flying,
In the fire
Guy dying.
Sparkling Roman
Candles sighing.
In the house,
Cat crying.

Coloured rocket
Tails soaring.
Writhing bonfire
Flames roaring.
Thoughtlessly with
Bangers warring,
Vivid memories
We're storing.

Catherine wheels
Sparking, spinning,
Crimson stars
In darkness winning.
Then at last
The crowd thinning,
Smokey eyed,
Goes home, grinning

Madeline Mayne

Autumn

Sweeping up leaves, I come
across a few dead blooms
I just don't remember
growing in summer – queer
pink-striped stalks; and some
purple cone shapes – mushrooms?
'Last week's Fifth November,'
I think, and all is clear.

Roy Fuller

View Over a Fence

Small sparrows light
on a thin
elm like Christmas
ornaments. I turn
the corner. They
leave the tree
dim
and undecorated.

Donna Wasiczko

35

Christmas Day in the Suburbs

How hushed the day is,
No one is around,
The streets are empty
There is hardly a sound.
The frost has touched the garden
With purifying white,
Even the birds are silent
And keeping out of sight,
As if they knew
It is a special day
When love came down
And goodness had its way.

John Cotton

Legend

Snow-blind the meadow; chiming ice
Struck at the wasted water's rim.
An infant in a stable lay.
A child watched for a sight of Him.

'I would have brought spring flowers,' she said.
'But where I wandered none did grow.'
Young Gabriel smiled, opened his hand,
And blossoms pierced the sudden snow.

She plucked the gold, the red, the green,
And with a garland entered in.
'What is your name?' Young Gabriel said.
The maid she answered, 'Magdalen.'

Charles Causley

Four Legends about Christmas Eve

Who was first to know the news?
  I, croaked the raven;
Flying high across the sky
Above the fields of Bethlehem,
When I saw, filled with awe,
  Angels at the Gates of Heaven!

Who wove a cover for his crib?
  I, sang the wren;
I flew around until I found
In the fields of Bethlehem
Bit by bit, enough to knit
  A blanket made of grass and moss.

Who warmed the baby with her breath?
  I, lowed the cow;
I warmed his bed within the shed
Beside the fields of Bethlehem,
And God blessed me so I would be
  The sweetest-breathed of animals.

Who was first to tell the news?
  I, called the cock;
I filled my chest and crowed my best
Across the fields of Bethlehem,
Throughout the night till it was light
  'Christ is born in Bethlehem!'

Brian Levison

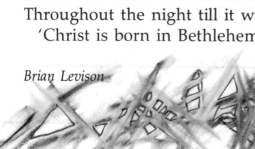

Cat and the Weather

Cat takes a look at the weather.
Snow.
Puts a paw on the sill.
His perch is piled, is a pillow.

Shape of his pad appears.
Will it dig? No.
Not like sand.
Like his fur almost.

But licked, not liked.
Too cold.
Insects are flying, fainting down.
He'll try

to bat one against the pane.
They have no body and no buzz.
And now his feet are wet;
it's a puzzle.

Shakes each leg,
then shakes his skin
to get the white flies off.
Looks for his tail,

tells it to come on in
by the radiator.
World's turned queer
somehow. All white,

no smell. Well, here
inside it's still familiar.
He'll go to sleep until
it puts itself right.

May Swenson

Blue Toboggans

scarves for the apaches
wet gloves for snowballs
whoops for white clouds
and blue toboggans

stamping for a tingle
lamps for four o'clock
steamed glass for buses
and blue toboggans

tuning-forks for Wenceslas
white fogs for Prestwick
mince pies for the Eventides
and blue toboggans

TV for the lonely
a long haul for heaven
a shilling for the gas
and blue toboggans

Edwin Morgan

Upon A Time

Once upon a time
The rain
Washed the trees
And bushes
And shrubs and grass.
It left
Flowers alone
In case their colours
Might run.

Once upon a time
The wind
Made its way
Across corn
And wheat
And barley.
It left birds
Alone so their wings
Wouldn't fold.

Once upon a time
Dawn came
And shone
On glass
On roofs
And playgrounds,
But it left
Shadow for fear
Night-time fade.

Once upon a time
Night darkened
Like an upturned
Bucket over everything.
In the bucket
Of night
There are holes
So light may
Leak through.

John Fairfax

All Change!

All change! All change!

When the guard on the train
or the bus conductor
shouts '*All change!*'
and everyone has to
grab their things
in a terrible fluster
and get out again –
just suppose
he was a magician in disguise
having a joke!
and the moment he spoke,
suddenly all the mums and dads
with their papers and cases and shopping-bags,
and school-children, workmen, office-girls neat
did change!
and found themselves
out in the street
like a runaway zoo –
with a bear or two,
a tiger, a goat, a wasp and a frog,
pigs, crows, snakes and a kangaroo-dog,
an alligator, a chimpanzee –
and a few left behind on board,
a sunflower,
a couple of stones
and a tree –

What do you think you'd be?

Libby Houston

Cloud Cuckoo

I am the sailor
who sails in a cloud
and fishes the mackerel
out of the sky.

I am the lamplighter
who lights up the stars
I gather the dewdrops
at dawn.

Mine is the palette
that colours the rainbow
and paints in a face
for the man in the moon.

I turn on the sun
rising and setting –
all right in my world
it works like a dream.

Michael Henry

How Far?

How far away
Is the evening star?
Ask the night horse
He knows how far.

Talk to him gently
Give him honey and hay
And seven bells for his bridle
And he will take you away.

Snorting white fire
He will stream through the air,
Past mountains of the moon
And the rainbow's stair.

And if you go singing
Through the dark and the cold
Your purse will be filled
With silver and gold.

Olive Dove

Poem of Solitary Delight

What a delight it is
When of a morning,
I get up and go out
To find in full bloom a flower
That yesterday was not there.

Tachibana Akemi

8 a.m. Shadows

Everyone's shadow is taller than really,
The shadows of giants are taller than trees,
The shadows of children are big as their parents,
And shadows of trotting dogs bend at the knees.
Everyone's shadow is taller than really,
Everyone's shadow is thinner than thin,
8 a.m. shadows are long as the dawning,
    Pulling the night away,
    Coaxing the light to say;
    'Welcome, all shadows,
    Day, please begin!'

Patricia Hubbell

Song

There once was a widow
who lived in a meadow.
She sat in the shadow
and cried all the day.
'Oh I'm so lonely,
I'm one and I'm only
so I sit in the shadow
and I cry all the day.'

There once was a widower,
no wife and no brother.
He lived in the shadow
and sorrowed all day.
'Oh I'm so lonely
for I am the only
one left of my people.
I sorrow all day.'

A traveller came riding,
told of the widow
who lived in the meadow
and cried all the day.
'Go down to the widow.
You'll find her in shadow.
Go courting the widow
in violet and grey.'

He married the widow
who lived in the shadow.
Now they're not grieving,
no longer alone.
They walk in the sunshine
through flowers in the meadow.
Forever together,
their sorrow is gone.

Miranda Harris

An old lady

An old lady
  sat under a tree
    on a hot summer's day.
     I see you like my shade
      said the tree.

On the contrary
  said the old lady
    I used to sit here &
     enjoy the sun when
      you were too small to

cast a shadow
  and I've been waiting
    for you to move ever
      since.

Paul Johnson

Green man in the garden

Green man in the garden
  Staring from the tree,
Why do you look so long and hard
  Through the pane at me?

Your eyes are dark as holly,
  Of sycamore your horns,
Your bones are made of elder-branch,
  Your teeth are made of thorns.

Your hat is made of ivy-leaf,
  Of bark your dancing shoes,
And evergreen and green and green
  Your jacket and shirt and trews.

Leave your house and leave your land
  And throw away the key,
And never look behind, he creaked
  And come and live with me.

I bolted up the window,
  I bolted up the door,
I drew the blind that I should find
  The green man never more.

But when I softly turned the stair
  As I went up to bed,
I saw the green man standing there.
  Sleep well, my friend, he said.

Charles Causley

Resolution at the New Year

Children drag home through dusk,
week-old snow brown in hedgerows,
a full moon slices the wood.

Somewhere spring is gathering its green,
star gives place to climbing star
(they too have grown older).

I shall not be careless this year:
I shall not forget to see the wild garlic blossom
– as I did last May, and the May before.

Frances Horovitz

Shrove Tuesday

Pancakes tossed
up and over
flipping like frisbees
popped out of the pan
batter blistered crisp
goldening to a turn.

Michael Henry

Three Days into March

Today
the birds sang
and yellow crocuses
opened wide their mouths
to feast on
sunlight.

Today
the sky cleared
and enthusiastic trees
stretched out their limbs
all thick with
promises.

Today
I stood still
and the greens, the blues
and the yellows clamoured
to dance behind
my eyes.

Moira Andrew

RAIN

RAIN –
crystals melting
shivering a shape
at one with the wind
spitting angry thoughts in faces
creating a moving green river of the lawn
swelling the streams to cleanse
the polluted banks of debris
rainbow thumbprints
on grey tarmac –
RAIN

Kay Cornish

The Singing Time

Plumtrees in orchards day and night
Make all the world a dream of white.

A thrush is throbbing in the copse
A jewelled song that never stops.

Bluebells in drifts of deep sapphire
Have set the ferny woods on fire.

A cuckoo calls his tune until
First shadows fall on field and hill.

Tulips in solid squads and teams
Are almost bursting at the seams.

A jenny wren with needle eyes
Is in the bushes catching flies.

So flowers and birds are in their prime,
These happy days, this singing time.

Leonard Clark

Tall Nettles

Tall nettles cover up, as they have done
These many springs, the rusty harrow, the plough
Long worn out, and the roller made of stone:
Only the elm butt tops the nettles now.

This corner of the farmyard I like most:
As well as any bloom upon a flower
I like the dust on the nettles, never lost
Except to prove the sweetness of a shower.

Edward Thomas

July Day Spectacular

I sit in the third row of
gray rocks upholstered
with lichen. Light pours
from the flies of heaven
on a thirty mile stage-set;
and there, by the footlights
of breaking water,
oystercatchers,
going through their old routines,
put on their black-and-white minstrel show
watched by a bandmaster pigeon
with built-in epaulettes.

Norman McCaig

crickets

Crickets
Talk
In the tall
Grass
All
Late summer
Long.
When
Summer
Is gone
The dry
Grass
Whispers
Alone.

Valerie Worth

59

Plot

Bramble
grows up
grows heavy
bows down,
knuckles
new soil
makes roots
makes loops
grows heavy
bows down
drops roots
lifts loops
with calm
tenacity
walks in
takes
over.

Pamela Gillilan

Autumn

A touch of cold in the autumn night —
I walked abroad,
And saw the ruddy moon lean over a hedge,
Like a red-faced farmer.
I did not stop to speak, but nodded,
And round about were the wistful stars
With white faces like town children

T. E. Hulme

The Elm-Tree

One November morning clean and cold
The elm-tree still was heavy with her gold,
Though beech and oak and aspen stripped and bare
Lifted their leafless branches in the air.

Then something happened, and her golden dress
The noble elm shook from her nakedness;
Yes, in a single hour, like a great rain,
She gave back all her leaves to earth again.

Eleanor Farjeon

The Ice Skaters

They merrily weave over the blue transparency,
Fir trees against snow-threatening sky etched
Nicely in, curvet, chassé, and slide

Merrily off – a long take, this time. I see them
Shining blonde and lustrous dark and honey-
coloured meet, escape, pirouette, and off again

Over the smooth hard sheen. Under their legs
Twirling so merrily what deep acres live
Of dark or weed or slow fish nudging past,

What bottom-sods of mud, what tangles of weed –
They slide over the surface, beckoning us on,
Gingerly we follow, test the security – fine,

They call, weaving away merrily. You
Venture to catch them up, reach out, and
Find yourself struggling in dirty water. Call,

Ice in your mouth, spluttering blindly down,
Down into the mud, entangling with weed you go.
Their laughter tinkles prettily over the ice.

Philip Hobsbaum

Three Dragons

One dragon is big, one is small,
One dragon has no size at all.

One guards a castle, one a cave
The last is witless no matter how brave.

The first is green and has golden teeth
Has spikes above and claws beneath,

Its mouth is red as the westering sun
And it saw things when the world begun.

One dragon is big, one is small,
One dragon has no size at all.

The small one longs to hear my song
And return me home where I belong.

It stays with me through winter night
And warms my heart until it's light.

This small dragon roars at lies
Because the world spins in its eyes.

One dragon is big, one is small,
One dragon has no size at all.

The last hums words in gentle air
And soothes away lamenting care.

It winks at me through blackest night
And fills each day with summer light.

This dragon has no size at all
Only a heart beat knows its call.

From my mirror three dragons stare
Each one claims my constant care.

They play along the calling day
And colour my eyes which way they may

Green if I envy, blue when I'm calm,
Dark when I'm lonely, grey for charm.

These three dragons I keep alone . . .
But maybe this song's for another one?

John Fairfax

Rabbit and Dragon

Not a fair comparison, really:
dragons don't live in hutches,
have shining scales, great eyelids
and burning breath. They don't
eat mash and meal at thirty-one pence a pound
from the petshop. They sleep
for long ages on beds of gold.
People don't make songs about them.

But rabbits don't
eat children.
And nobody hunts them with bright spears.

I'd rather be a dragon
but rabbit's easier.

Tony Charles

A Small Dragon

I've found a small dragon in the woodshed.
Think it must have come from deep inside a forest
because it's damp and green and leaves
are still reflecting in its eyes.

I fed it on many things, tried grass,
the roots of stars, hazel-nut and dandelion,
but it stared up at me as if to say, I need
food you can't provide.

It made a nest among the coal,
not unlike a bird's but larger,
it is out of place here
and is quite silent.

If you believed in it I would come
hurrying to your house to let you share my wonder,
but I want instead to see
if you yourself will pass this way.

Brian Patten

Bananas

It may be
necessary to hang upside
down from a tree
to get a new
perspective. Then you can
see that grass grows
up. What a dance
to measure lizard
jumps and spider
dangles at eye
level! To hear
birds fly
over your feet –
match shadows to faces,
feathers to wings,
footsteps to eyes.

Donna Wasiczko

Dream Variation

To fling my arms wide
In some place of the sun,
To whirl and to dance
Till the white day is done.
Then rest at cool evening
Beneath a tall tree
While night comes on gently,
  Dark like me –
That is my dream!

To fling my arms wide
In the face of the sun,
Dance! Whirl! Whirl!
Till the quick day is done.
Rest at pale evening . . .
A tall, slim tree . . .
Night coming tenderly
  Black like me.

Langston Hughes

Nature

We have neither summer or winter
Neither autumn nor spring
We have instead the days
When gold sun shines on the lush green canefield
Magnificently.

The days when the rain beats like bullets on the roofs
And there is no sound but the swish of water in the
   gullies,
And trees struggling in the high Jamaica winds . . .

Part of a poem by *H. D. Carberry*

Michael

The worm is worried about the blackbird,
the blackbird is worried about the cat.
But the cat, the cat has no worries
sleeps, paw twitching in long feline dreams
as only well-fed carnivores can sleep
comfortable and uncamouflaged on hedge cuttings
as where the duvet indents for him,
wakes to snap at butterflies
for being there
for having wings
for clouding up his sky.

Part of a poem by *Elaine Eveleigh*

Chameleon

I can think sharply
and I can change:
my colours cover a considerable range.

I can be some mud by
an estuary,
I can be a patch on the bark of a tree.

I can be green grass
or a little thin stone
– or if I really want to be left alone,

I can be a shadow . . .
What I am on your
multi-coloured bedspread, I am not quite sure.

Alan Brownjohn

Robin

There's blood on the mat.
Has that cat
Caught my bird?
Eaten it?
I shall worry until evening.
Will the song
That for an hour long
Till sunset fills the garden
Still be heard?

You can't give cats
A briefing;
Kill rats,
It's nice to eat mice
But in a word
WICKED
To finish off a bird.

Pamela Gillilan

The Bird Fancier

Up to his shoulders
In grasses coarse as silk,
The white cat with the yellow eyes
Sits with all four paws together,
Tall as a quart of milk.

He hardly moves his head
To touch with nice nose
What his wary whiskers tell him
Is here a weed
And here a rose.

On a dry stick he rubs his jaws,
And the thin
Corners of his smile
Silently mew when a leaf
Tickles his chin.

With a neat grimace
He nips a new
Blade of feathery grass,
Flicks from his ear
A grain of dew.

His sleepy eyes are wild with birds,
Every sparrow, thrush and wren
Widens their furred horizons
Till their flying song
Narrows them again.

James Kirkup

True

When
the green eyes
of a cat
look deep into
you

you know
that
whatever it is
they are saying
is
true.

Lilian Moore

Cat

I am a cat
an old Egyptian cat
an old old cat.
My prim stone haunches
rooted in Nile dust.
My strange soft eyes
looking inward
towards a pin-point
of eternity.

Patricia Pogson

Mr Jonas is Cool

Jonas is back
bristling his black furry tail and arching
his long tight body over pointed feet in
a new way

He didn't leap, shooting ladders across
my new tights
or such and gnaw at my hair
or shove his little wet black nose into my face
giving me hay-fever

while I had cried lost for days
through mazes of fenced gardens

He just strolled back to his pad
for a break, glutted
with birds.

Jeni Couzyn

The Prayer of the Little Ducks who Went into the Ark

Dear God,
give us a flood of water,
Let it rain tomorrow and always,
Give us plenty of little slugs
and other luscious things to eat.
Protect all folk who quack
and everyone who knows how to swim.
Amen.

Carmen Bernos de Gasztold
A Portuguese poem translated by Rumer Godden.

Frogs

Frogs sit more solid
Than anything sits. In mid-leap they are
Parachutists falling
In a free fall. They die on roads
With arms across their chests and
Heads high.

I love frogs that sit
Like Buddha, that fall without
Parachutes, that die
Like Italian tenors.

Above all, I love them because,
Pursued in water, they never
Panic so much that they fail
To make stylish triangles
With their ballet dancer's
Legs.

Norman McCaig

An Alphabet of Questions

Have Angleworms attractive homes?
Do Bumblebees have brains?
Do Caterpillars carry combs?
Do Dodos dote on drains?
Can Eels elude electric earls?
Do Flatfish fish for flats?
Are Grigs agreeable to girls?
Do Hares have hunting hats?
Do ices make an Ibex ill?
Do Jackdaws jug their jam?
Do Kites kiss all the kids they kill?
Do Llamas live on lamb?
Will Moles molest a mounted mink?
Do Newts deny the news?
Are Oysters boisterous when they drink?
Do Parrots prowl in pews?
Do Quakers get their quills from quails?
Do Rabbits rob on roads?
Are Snakes supposed to sneer at snails?
Do Tortoises eat toads?
Can Unicorns perform on horns?
Do Vipers value veal?
Do Weasels weep when fast asleep?
Can Xylophagans squeal?
Do Yaks in packs invite attacks?
Are Zebras full of zeal?

Charles Edward Carryl

Candle

I had a crooked candle
in a wooden dish.
It leaped and it flounced
like a little eager fish,
it turned to the left side –
it turned to the right –
it bowed and it blustered
and wished me 'Good night!'

I had a crooked candle
in a wooden stand,
as bold and as gold
as any in the land.
It waxed and it wavered,
it stretched and it shone
with lightness
             and brightness
till darkness
             had gone.

Jean Kenward

The Magical Mouse

I am the magical mouse
I don't eat cheese
I eat sunsets
And the tops of trees

I don't wear fur

I wear funnels
Of lost ships and the weather
That's under dead leaves
I am the magical mouse

I don't fear cats

Or woodowls
I do as I please
Always
I don't eat crusts
I am the magical mouse
I eat
Little birds and maidens

That taste like dust

Kenneth Patchen

The Gingerbread Lady

The gingerbread lady's
A bitter old maid, she's
Possessed of a terrible hunger.
She watches the girls
And the boys with crisp curls
Getting younger and younger and younger.

She pebbles her rooftop
With pastille and gob-stop
And gums by the dime and the dozen.
Smarties galore
Make a path to her door
Behind which she's stoking her oven.

Though her features are merry,
In desperate hurry
Her heart and her stomach are rumbling
O alas and alack,
Down the dark forest track
You can hear the poor children come tumbling

John Mole

The Ghoul

The gruesome ghoul, the grisly ghoul,
without the slightest noise
waits patiently beside the school
to feast on girls and boys.

He lunges fiercely through the air
as they come out to play,
then grabs a couple by the hair
and drags them far away.

He cracks their bones and snaps their backs
and squeezes out their lungs,
he chews their thumbs like candy snacks
and pulls apart their tongues.

He slices their stomachs and bites their hearts
and tears their flesh to shreds,
he swallows their toes like toasted tarts
and gobbles down their heads.

Fingers, elbows, hands and knees
and arms and legs and feet —
he eats them with delight and ease,
for every part's a treat.

And when the gruesome, grisly ghoul
has nothing left to chew,
he hurries to another school
and waits . . . perhaps for you.

Jack Prelutsky

Late

You're late, said miss.
The bell has gone,
dinner numbers done
and work begun.

What have you got to say for yourself?

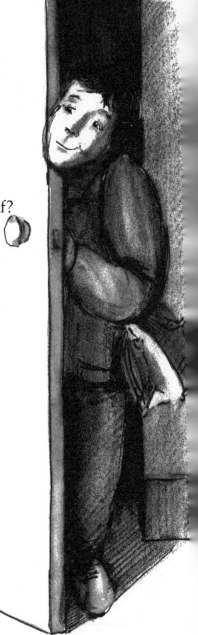

Well, it's like this, miss.
Me mum was sick,
me dad fell down the stairs,
the wheel fell of me bike,
and then we lost our Billy's snake
behind the kitchen chairs. Earache
struck down me grampy, me gran
took quite a funny turn.
Then on the way I met this man
whose dog attacked me shin –
look miss, you can see the blood,
it doesn't look too good,
does it?

Yes, yes, sit down –
and next time say you're sorry
for disturbing all the class.
Now get on with your story,
fast!

Please miss, I've got nothing to write about.

Judith Nicholls

Wet Playtime

Draughts again
not through the door
but hopping like fleas
over this board.

Bored stiff again
drummed into our seats
by the grey rain drilling
holes in the windows.

Pains in our heads
from reading old comics
that fall apart
with tattered laughter.

The long day stretches
and yawns until hometime,
then jumps through the puddles
splashing all the world.

David Harmer

Janitor Jeffries

Janitor Jeffries
bucket & mops
scrub
polish
wipe
never stops

Janitor Jeffries
cleaning the stair
tiles
steps &
window
in long underwear

Janitor Jeffries
up before dawn
wheeze
cough &
splutter
expression forlorn

Janitor Jeffries
bike in the rain
hills
puddles
splash
'gain and again

Janitor Jeffries
August arrives
your marks,
steady
go!
two weeks in St. Ives

Janitor Jeffries
feet in the sea
ice
cream &
winkles
o golly o me

Janitor Jeffries
a fortnight's delight
case
hat &
tickets
back Sunday night

Janitor Jeffries
bucket & mops
scrub
polish
wipe
never stops.

Peter Mortimer

Batman

Batman
Age 10½
Patrols the streets of his suburb
At night
Between seven and eight-o-clock.
If he is out later than this
he is spanked
and sent to bed
without supper.

Batman
Almost 11
Patrols the streets of his suburb
At night
After he has finished his homework.

Batman,
His freckles
And secret identity
protected
By the mask and cloak
His Auntie Elsie
made on her sewing machine,
Patrols
At night
Righting wrongs.

Tonight he is on the trail of
Raymond age 11
(large for his age)
Who has stolen Stephen's
Gobstoppers and football cards.

Batman
Patrolling the streets of his suburb
righting wrongs
Finds Raymond,
Demands the return of the stolen goods.
Raymond knocks him over,
Rips his mask,
Tears his cloak,
And steals his utility belt.
Batman starts to cry,
Wipes his eyes with his cape.
(His hankie was in the belt).

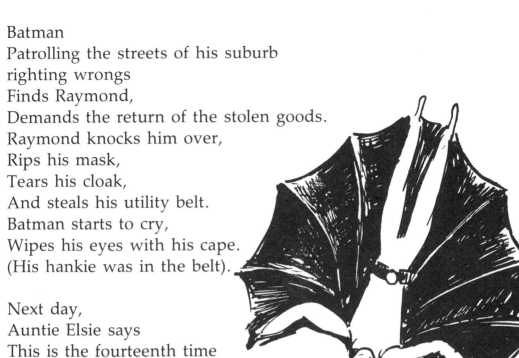

Next day,
Auntie Elsie says
This is the fourteenth time
I've had to mend your
Batman costume.
If it happens again
You'll have to whistle for it.

Batman
Eats a bag of crisps.

John Turner

The Spaceman

Under the royal scent of the lilac tree,
When the rain was still moist and calm,
A rainbow man walked towards me,
Cupping sunbeams in his palm.

He had staring eyes of marigold,
With pupils neat as a pin,
His suit had buttons of shimmering gold,
And his voice was textured and thin.

He held out his hand like flowers,
And my fingers changed their hue,
As I traced the dancing colours,
Red, green, yellow, and indigo blue.

He led me to his spaceship,
Near the barn with old oak beams,
And we travelled the rays of the rainbow,
In search of forgotten dreams.

Kay Cornish

Uncle Terry was a skydiver

Uncle Terry was a skydiver.
He liked best
the earth spread out beneath him
like a springcleaned counterpane.
The wind his safety net.

He free fell every day
and liked it so much
he decided to stay.
And they say he's still there
sunbathing in the air.

He sleeps each night
tucked up in moonlight
wakes at dawn
and chases clouds.

Living off the food birds bring

Uncle Terry on the wing

away   from   it   all

dizzy   with   joy

Roger McGough

Father says

Father says
Never
let
me
see
you
doing
that
again
father says
tell you once
tell you a thousand times
come hell or high water
his finger drills my shoulder
never let me see you doing that again

My brother knows all his phrases off by heart
so we practise them in bed at night.

Michael Rosen

When my Dad Came Home from the Sea

My dad came home from the sea
in 1958.
He walked up the garden path
wearing a sailor's hat
and he forgot to close the gate.

My mam had said to me
'Your dad is leaving the sea'
and I thought of the sea
being left on its own.

I was sitting in my chair
when my dad came home from the sea.
He smiled and spoke to me,
and took off his sailor's hat.
He smiled at me, and I smiled
when my dad came home from the sea.

Ian McMillan

My Papa's Waltz

The whiskey on your breath
Could make a small boy dizzy;
But I hung on like death:
Such waltzing was not easy.

We romped until the pans
Slid from the kitchen shelf;
My mother's countenance
Could not unfrown itself.

The hand that held my wrist
Was battered on one knuckle;
At every step you missed
My right ear scraped a buckle.

You beat time on my head
With a palm caked hard by dirt,
Then waltzed me off to bed
Still clinging to your shirt.

Theodore Roethke

At Peace

For Eric and Colin

The boat was asleep on the sea,
   Its anchor chain taut.
The crew, only Billy and me,
     Were cleaning the fish we had caught:
       Scraping the scales,
       Removing the entrails,
And tossing them over the sides
   To starboard and port.

The ocean was also asleep,
   Its waters were still.
We gazed at the blue of the deep
     Through the green of the frill.
       I said not a word.
       And yet Billy heard:
He looked up at me and he smiled,
   And I smiled at Bill.

The sun was now high in the sky
   And climbing still higher;
A mild breeze was making a try
     At containing this fire;
       And there on the sea
       Sat Billy and me,
Encrusted with salt from the spray
   And salt we'd perspired.

We sat there, both tranquil, alone,
    Serene as could be;
Each seat of wood was a throne
    For the kings of the sea;
        Gentle and slow
        We rocked to and fro;
Out there we were chained to the boat,
    But we knew we were free.

Felix Redmill

Exploring the Rock Pool

We explore the rock pool
A small world of its own:
The scuttling crab, quick shrimps,
Sea-polished stone
With hints of colours
Enhanced by the light –
Refracting water
Making all so bright,
The strands of seaweed
Verdant, sleek as silk,
The tiny limpets
Shells as white as milk.
A sea in miniature
Which lasts for just a day,
When the tide renews it
Washing the old away.

John Cotton

The Round Pond

Ducks squat at the edge of clouds.
Kites glide stealthily like pikes.
A white yacht makes a voyage
To nowhere. Two small boys
Poke sticks into their jelly likenesses.
Parents, dogs, foreigners, predatory
Girls stand round the pond
Like minutes on a clock.

Vicki Feaver

The hardest thing in the world to do

The hardest thing in the world to do
is to stand in the hot sun
at the end of a long queue for ice-creams
watching all the people who've just bought theirs
coming away from the queue
giving their ice-creams their very first lick.

Michael Rosen

Three-Hole

Three-hole
is the name
of a marble game
we got in Guyana.

Is fun to play
and not hard.
Just dig three lil holes
in you yard
or the sand
by you gate.
Then aim straight

for first-hole
    second-hole
        third-hole.

If you lucky
and you marble
go in all the holes
one two three

Then is you chance
to knock you friend marble.
Send it flying for a dance.
When marble burst then fun start.

John Agard

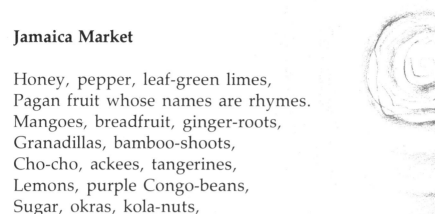

Jamaica Market

Honey, pepper, leaf-green limes,
Pagan fruit whose names are rhymes.
Mangoes, breadfruit, ginger-roots,
Granadillas, bamboo-shoots,
Cho-cho, ackees, tangerines,
Lemons, purple Congo-beans,
Sugar, okras, kola-nuts,
Citrons, hairy coconuts,
Fish, tobacco, native hats,
Gold bananas, woven mats,
Plantains, wild-thyme, pallid leeks,
Pigeons with their scarlet beaks,
Oranges and saffron yams,
Baskets, ruby guava jams,
Turtles, goat-skins, cinnamon,
Allspice, conch-shells, golden rum.
Black skins, babel — and the sun
That burns all colours into one.

Agnes Maxwell-Hall

Fiesta Melons

In Benidorm there are melons,
Whole donkey-carts full

Of innumerable melons,
Ovals and balls,

Bright green and thumpable
Laced over with stripes

Of turtle-dark green.
Choose an egg-shape, a world-shape,

Bowl one homeward to taste
in the whitehot noon:

Cream-smooth honeydews,
Pink-pulped whoppers,

Bump-rinded cantaloupes
With orange cores.

Sylvia Plath

Song of the Pop Bottles

Pop bottles pop-bottles
  In pop shops;
The pop-bottles Pop bottles
  Poor Pop drops.

When Pop drops pop-bottles,
  Pop-bottles plop!
Pop-bottle-tops topple!
  Pop mops slop!

Stop! Pop'll drop bottle!
  Stop, Pop, stop!
When Pop bottles pop-bottles,
  Pop-bottles pop!

Morris Bishop

The Greedy Giant

There was once a giant
So far from compliant,
    He wouldn't eat toast with his tea.
'A substance so horrid
Brings pains in my forehead,
    And aches in my toe-toes,' said he, said he,
    'And aches in my toe-toes,' said he.

They brought him a tartlet
To cheer up his heartlet,
    They brought him both jelly and jam;
But still while he gobbled,
He sighed and he sobbled,
    'You *don't* know how hungry I am, I am,
    You don't *know* how hungry I am!'

They brought him a cruller
To make him feel fuller,
    They brought him some pancakes beside,
They brought him a muffin,
On which he was stuffin',
    When all of a sudden he died, he died,
    When all of a sudden he died.

Laura E. Richards

Rhymes for a Blue-Bottle

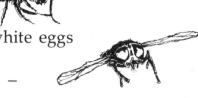

Some mother or other laid a load of white eggs
    In a rotten bit of food,
And that's how I came into the world –
    And it tasted rich and good!

We had no teeth and we had no legs,
    But we turned the stuff to a soup,
And slopped and wallowed and sucked the dregs,
    Our maggoty family group!

We squirmed in our supper, we twirled in our tea,
    Till we could grow no fatter,
Then we all dropped off to sleep – now that was
    The strangest part of the matter,

For we went quite hard, and brown, like pods,
    And when it was time to rise,
Blow me if we hadn't been born again
    With wings, this time, like – flies!

O I'm buzzing and blue and beautiful,
    I'm an ace at picking and stealing!
I've got masses of eyes to see you with,
    And legs to run on your ceiling!

What's in the dustbin smelling so rare?
    I'm zooming in to see,
Then I'm coming to dance on your dinner – look sharp,
    You'll find no flies on me!

Libby Houston

The Witch's Brew

Hubble bubble at the double
Cooking pot stir up some trouble.

Into my pot
There now must go
Leg of lamb
And a green frog's toe,

Old men's socks
And dirty jeans,
A rotten egg
And cold baked beans.

Hubble bubble at the double
Cooking pot stir up some trouble.

One dead fly
And a wasp's sting,
The eye of a sheep
And the heart of a king;

A stolen jewel
And mouldy salt,
And for good flavour
A jar of malt.

Hubble bubble at the double
Cooking pot stir up some trouble.

Wing of bird
and head of mouse,
Screams and howls
From that haunted house.

And don't forget
The jug of blood
Or the sardine tin,
Or the clod of mud.

Hubble bubble at the double
Cooking pot stir up some trouble!

Wes Magee

Question and Answer

Where do the days go
When you are young?
Where does a song go
Once it is sung?

When you are young
There are days without end
The song will return
On the lips of a friend.

Where do the birds go
When summer's done?
How fast is a rabbit
When on the run?

Birds after summer
To other lands roam
As fast as the rabbit
Can safely reach home.

Where would you hide
A particular stone?
Why, on the beach
Then it won't be alone.

How can you count
All the castles in Spain?
Twice on your fingers
Then check them again.

Eric Slayter

Questions

What is it about a white horse
Beneath a grey sky?
What is it about his lumpy, solid head
Munching grass?
Is it the green of wet grass?
Is it the halt in my busy journey
To watch him eat wet grass?
Is it all the white horses
Through history,
And all the men who have stopped,
With brushes, cameras, or words,
Or wordlessly, for whatever
It is about a white horse
Munching wet grass
Beneath a grey sky
That makes men stop, and ask,
What is it about a white horse
Munching green grass
Beneath a grey sky?

Malcolm Povey

A Memory

This I remember
I saw from a train
A shaggy wild pony
That stood in the rain.

Where I was going,
And where was the train,
I cannot remember,
I cannot explain.

All these years after
It comes back again:
A shaggy wild pony
That stood in the rain.

Douglas Gibson

The Tunnel

The tunnel's long finger
pokes a hole through the hillside.

It wiggles around
gouging the dark out.

The men who built it
are all dead now,
they tunnel the dark earth.

The steam that scorched
fumes on the brickwork
is now exhausted.

Prodding and pushing,
the tunnel worms right through the rock

pouring trains down its throat
like silver liquid.

David Harmer

Bus Route

When the bus is full
it creeps uphill
like an old man climbing
the stairs to bed.

Down the other side
it rumbles into town
barging through the traffic,
an angry bully.

Out in the country
the bus is empty
rattling through the quiet lanes
humming softly.

But it can never stay;
it has to push and shove,
bruise and scrape its skin
in the rough and tumble town.

Surging crowds of people
swarm and clamber on it,
fill it to the top
at the bottom of the hill.

David Harmer

The First Bus of the Day

I'm the first bus of the day,
always up before the sun.

In the dark depot
the driver sits inside me half asleep.
The cleaner sweeps my seats.
The inspector kicks my tyres
to make sure I'm awake
then he turns the numbers on my face
and it's out of the depot into the street,

I'm the first bus of the day,
always up before the sun.

George Inkerman

At the Bus Stop

Ten are queueing in the rain.
One decides to go by train.
Nine are waiting – drenched and late
Taxi stops and now there're eight.
Still they stay. 'Where IS eleven?'
One walks off and now there're seven.
Grumpy. Tense. They start to curse.
One jumps on a passing hearse.
Now the six united wail
Then impatient, one turns tail.
Five infuriated folk
Cough and sneeze and wheeze and croak
'I can't stand this any more,'
Someone cries, and now there're four.
Sports car stops with shiny bonnet
'Right. Here goes,' and one lands on it.
Three are left, bereft and glum
Praying that the bus will come.
One despairing, thumbs a ride.
Only two remain outside.
'Coffee?' 'What a good idea!'
He and she then disappear.

'Drive on Charlie.' 'No queue.' 'Strange.'
'Well I guess it makes a change!'

Margaret Holmes

Journey Home

I remember the long homeward ride, begun
By the light that slanted in from the level sun;
And on the far embankment, in sunny heat,
Our whole train's shadow travelling, dark and complete.

A farmer snored. Two loud gentlemen spoke
Of the cricket and news. The pink baby awoke
And gurgled awhile. Till slowly out of the day
The last light sank in glimmer and ashy-grey.

I remember it all; and dimly remember, too,
The place where we changed – the dark trains lumbering
                                                through;
The refreshment-room, the crumbs and the slopped tea;
And the salt on my face, not of tears, not tears, but the sea.

Our train at last! Said Father, 'Now tumble in!
It's the last lap home!' And I wondered what 'lap' could
                                                mean;
But the rest is all lost, for a huge drowsiness crept
Like a yawn upon me; I leant against Mother and slept.

John Walsh

Trip to London

By seven o'clock we were on our way
by train to London for the day,
four hours of travelling in the sun,
arrived in rain at Paddington
with neighbours, friends, mother and me,
and everyone had come to see
the big shops and the well-known sights,
the famous streets with all their lights.

We strolled together everywhere,
fed pigeons in Trafalgar Square
who did not mind the drizzle there,
watched snorting traffic whizzing by,
waved at old Nelson standing high,
then sloshed our way to Waterloo
and, after lunch, went to the Zoo;
we managed to spend half an hour
learning history at the Tower
and just had time to see Hyde Park,
Buckingham Palace through the dark,
and going back I fell asleep
having no need for counting sheep.

We got back home at half-past eleven
and glad I was but still thanked heaven
for all I'd done and all I'd seen
though wished that I had met the Queen,
but never once shall I forget
slopping round London in the wet,
glad to be back with country things,
the trees and hills and murmurings
of bees in fields, birds on trees,
and rambling free and at my ease
whether in sun or whirling snow,
and all the people whom I know.

Leonard Clark

Changing Times

Many things are changing
Today in London Town
New buildings going up
Old ones coming down
Just like London people
Houses too grow old
And can no longer do their job
To keep out damp and cold
Many are old fashioned
And were built long ago
For people in a different age
Who didn't hurry so
People's ways are changing
Like the things we use
Telephones for speaking
Television news
Just try to imagine
How things used to be

Different songs to listen to
Different things to see
Everyone used horses
Or else their own two feet
Everything moved slowly
Like the policeman on his beat
No motor cars to take them
Quickly on their way
No discos or videos
Like there are today
No package holidays
And no aeroplanes
No electric railways
And only puffer trains
People used to manage
It didn't matter how
But when you come to think of it
Aren't you glad it's NOW.

Eric Slayter

Open Windows

The windows are open at Number One,
And Dick the canary sings in the sun.

On her piano, little Miss Moore
Practises scales at Number Four.

A kettle is whistling at Number Ten.
Old Mother Moon's making tea again.

At Number Sixteen young Jenny is in;
There's her transistor's happy din!

The window at Number Eighteen is wide;
You can hear Mrs. Chadwick coughing inside.

Tapping his typewriter all the day through,
Mr. Gray's working at Twenty-two.

But here's Thirty-three. We hurry on past.
The curtains are drawn and the windows shut fast.

It's dark and unfriendly, cheerless and chill
– And a lean cat sleeps on the window-sill.

Alexander Franklin

Our Street

Our street is not a posh place,
Say the mums in curlers, dads in braces, kids in nothing.
Our street is not a quiet place,
Says the football match, our honking bikes, our shouts.
Our street is not a tidy place,
Say the lolly wrapper, chippie bags, and written-on
      walls.
Our street is not a lazy place,
Says the car washing dads, clothes washing mums, and
      marbling boys.
Our street is not a new place,
Say the paint-peeled doors, pavements worn, and
      crumbly walls.
Our street is not a green place,
Say the pavements grey, forgotten gardens, lines of cars.
But our street is the best
Says me.

L. T. Baynton

INDEX OF FIRST LINES